Russell Wilson

By Jon M. Fishman

AMAZING ATHLETES

Lerner Publications • Minneapolis

Lerner Publications Company
A division of Lerner Publishing Group, Inc.
241 First Avenue North
Minneapolis, MN 55401 USA

For reading levels and more information, look up this title at www.lernerbooks.com.

Library of Congress Cataloging-in-Publication Data

Fishman, Jon M.
      Russell Wilson / by Jon M. Fishman.
          pages   cm. — (Amazing athletes)
      Includes index.
      ISBN 978–1–4677–3675–6 (lib. bdg. : alk. paper)
      ISBN 978–1–4677–4589–5 (EB pdf)
          1. Wilson, Russell, 1988– 2. Football players—United States—Biography—Juvenile literature.
    3. Quarterbacks (Football)—United States—Biography—Juvenile literature. I. Title.
    GV939.W545F57 2015
    796.332092—dc23 [B]   2014009375

Manufactured in the United States of America
2 – BP – 3/1/15

TABLE OF CONTENTS

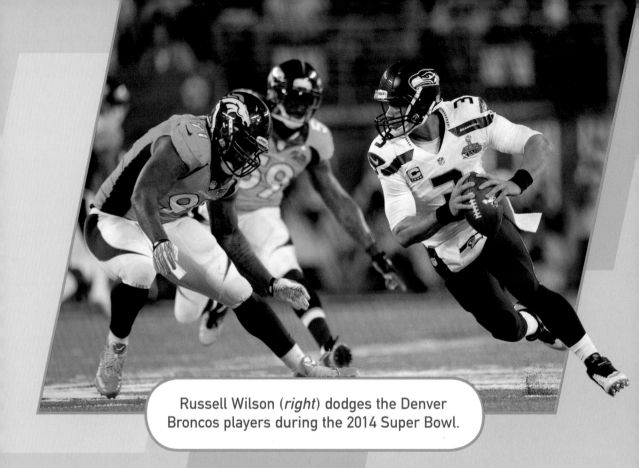

Russell Wilson (*right*) dodges the Denver Broncos players during the 2014 Super Bowl.

SUPER SEAHAWK

Russell Wilson and the Seattle Seahawks were crushing the Denver Broncos. The score was 29–0. Games in the National Football League (NFL) usually aren't so one-sided. The biggest game of the year almost never is.

The two teams were playing in the 2014 Super Bowl. Seattle had scored early and often. But Russell knew that he and his teammates couldn't relax. Peyton Manning and the Broncos usually score a lot of points. Russell planned to keep on scoring. The young **quarterback** wanted to put the game away.

Russell runs the ball out of bounds as he avoids the Broncos' defense.

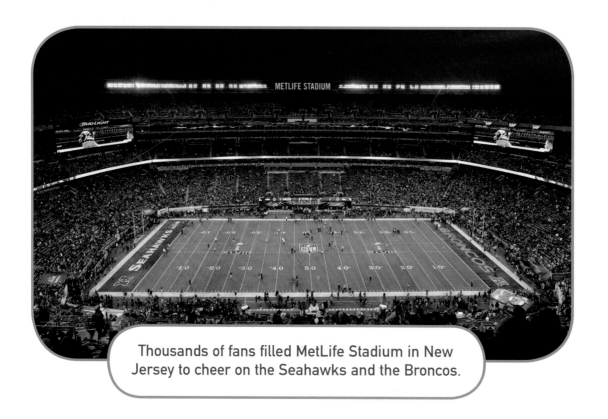

Thousands of fans filled MetLife Stadium in New Jersey to cheer on the Seahawks and the Broncos.

The Seahawks had the ball midway through the third quarter. Russell drove his team down the field. Then he fired a pass to Jermaine Kearse. The **wide receiver** caught the ball and broke a tackle. Then he busted out of another tackle. Denver **defenders** seemed to bounce off Kearse. He ran all the way for a touchdown!

Seattle didn't ease up when they got the ball again. Russell hit Doug Baldwin for yet another score. Both teams knew that Denver wouldn't have time to catch up. A few minutes later, Russell helped dump a bucket of Gatorade over his head coach. It was time to celebrate!

When the game clock finally ran out, the score was 43–8.

Russell throws the ball toward a Seahawks wide receiver.

Russell (*second from right*) and his teammates dump Gatorade on head coach Pete Carroll as they celebrate their victory.

Seattle had won one of the most lopsided games in Super Bowl history. Reporters streamed onto the field. Many of them wanted to talk to the young quarterback—the same quarterback who many people had thought was too short to play in the NFL.

Russell was on top of the NFL world in just his second season. But he wasn't surprised he had made it so far so quickly. He knows that if he plays his best, good things happen. "At the end of the day, you want to play your best football and that is what we did today," he said.

Reporters swarm the Seahawks after the team's Super Bowl win.

Russell (*right*) was an energetic kid from the start.

CHIPS OFF THE BLOCK

Harrison Wilson III and his wife, Tammy, welcomed a new child to the family on November 29, 1988. Russell Carrington Wilson is the couple's second son. His big brother, Harrison Wilson IV (also known as Harry), was born about six years before Russell. Everyone calls him Harry. Russell and Harry also have a younger sister named Anna.

Tammy and Harrison raised their children in Richmond, Virginia. The Wilsons are a very athletic family. Harry played lots of sports, including football. Russell loved to throw passes to his brother, even when the younger boy was just four years old. Anna is the star **point guard** on her high school basketball team.

Russell lived in Richmond, one of the oldest cities in Virginia.

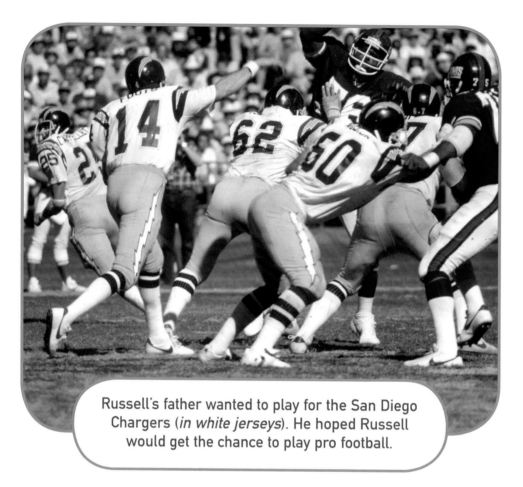

Russell's father wanted to play for the San Diego Chargers (*in white jerseys*). He hoped Russell would get the chance to play pro football.

The Wilson children take after their father when it comes to sports. Harrison had played football and baseball at Dartmouth College in New Hampshire. After college, he tried out for the NFL's San Diego Chargers. He didn't make the team, though.

Harrison encouraged his children to play sports. Before work, he would drive the boys to nearby fields to practice. But Harrison wanted his children to have a good education more than anything. He had earned a law **degree** at the University of Virginia. He wanted his children to have the same opportunity to succeed.

Russell and his brother and sister were happy and healthy. But when he was 13 years old, Russell learned that not all was well with his father. Harrison was driving his son to a youth baseball game. Suddenly, he passed out behind the wheel of the car.

Russell's sister, Anna, is one of the best young point guards in the country. "Thing I'm worried about, she may be taller than me [someday]," Russell said.

Russell had to take control of the car. "I had no idea what I was doing," he said. "We were in the middle of the highway. I pulled over at a stoplight. I got out of the car and ran to a car in front of me."

An ambulance came and took Harrison to the hospital. Russell learned that his father had **diabetes**. The disease would be a major part of the Wilson family life for years to come.

Russell played football at Collegiate School as a teenager.

"A KING IN EVERY CROWD"

In 2003, Russell started high school at Collegiate School in Richmond. As a first-year student, he still liked to play many sports. But football and baseball were his favorites.

That year, his dad taught him an important lesson. Harrison gave Russell a piece of paper.

Russell's dad (*right*) gave Russell the encouragement he needed to play his best.

It said, "There's a king in every crowd." Russell took the message to heart. "You never know what coach is watching you," he said. "You never know if there's a little kid in the stands who wants to be just like you."

Russell became the **varsity** team's starting quarterback in his sophomore season. He worked hard during every practice and game.

Russell helped make his high school football team the best in the state in 2005. They had a perfect record of 11–0 and won the state title. He threw for an amazing 40 touchdown passes. He also ran for 15 more touchdowns. He was named the *Richmond Times-Dispatch* Player of the Year in Virginia high school football. Russell also starred on the baseball diamond as his team's starting **shortstop**.

By the time Russell was a high school senior, he had proved that he was one of the best athletes in Virginia.

Russell played both football and baseball in high school.

He was ready for the next level. But many schools, such as the University of Virginia, didn't think Russell was tall enough to play quarterback in college. He is 5 feet 11 inches tall. Most college and NFL quarterbacks are well over 6 feet tall.

Charlie McFall was Russell's high school football coach. He was sure the young man could play quarterback on any team. "I don't really know anything about the college game other than the fact Russell's a quarterback, and I know what a special leader he is," Coach McFall said.

Russell's grandfather, Dr. Harrison B. Wilson Jr., was once the president of Norfolk State University in Virginia.

Fans of North Carolina State University's football team flock to Carter-Finley Stadium.

RUNNING WITH THE WOLFPACK

Russell was sure he wanted to play football in college. He also wanted to continue his baseball career. "I knew my whole life I wanted to play two sports in college," he said. He chose North Carolina (NC) State University.

The school let Russell play baseball and football. Even better, it agreed to give him a shot to play quarterback.

Russell began his college football career

with the NC State Wolfpack on the bench. He was a **redshirt** during the 2007 football season. That meant he couldn't play in games. Instead, he practiced and worked out and learned as much as he could.

Russell drops back to pass against the University of Maryland during a 2008 game in College Park, Maryland.

When the Wolfpack football team began practicing for the 2008 season, they didn't have a starting quarterback. Russell and three other players competed for the job. Russell beat out the competition and took the prize. He threw 17 touchdown passes for the season. He allowed only one **interception** all year.

Russell's first year playing college football was a huge success. He impressed people despite a busy schedule. Russell took a heavy class load and got good grades. He also played baseball in the spring and summer. That meant he missed a lot of practice time with the football team.

One day, Russell hopes to be a sports reporter. "I was never a cartoon guy," he said. "I was always watching ESPN."

"He would miss the spring [football] practices," said Wolfpack teammate J. R. Sweezy. "Like all of a spring. Then he would come in and know the offense better than the quarterbacks who had been there all spring. It was amazing he could fit it all in."

Russell brings the heat as a pitcher for NC State.

The young quarterback had become a star on both the football and baseball fields. Many people thought his future lay in baseball, though. In 2009, the Colorado Rockies chose Russell in the Major League Baseball (MLB) **draft**.

The day after the MLB draft, Russell visited his dad in the hospital. Harrison's health had not improved. He died during his son's visit. "I knew my dad heard me and he could hear everything I was telling him about how I got drafted," Russell said. "He was waiting for something great to happen. That's how I knew he went in peace."

Russell watches a 2010 loss to the Clemson Tigers. He doesn't let losses keep him down for long. That's a lesson he learned from his dad.

Russell runs in a touchdown for the University of Wisconsin during a 2011 game.

OUTPLAYING HIS SIZE

By 2011, Russell had earned his degree from NC State. But college football rules let him play for another year. Russell decided to switch schools. He went to the University of Wisconsin.

Russell became the starting quarterback right away. He and his teammates had an amazing year. They won their **conference** and played in the Rose Bowl. Wisconsin lost to the University of Oregon in a close game, 45–38.

After four seasons of college football, it was time for Russell to move on. He was going out on top. He'd thrown an unbelievable 33 touchdown passes with just four interceptions during the 2011 season.

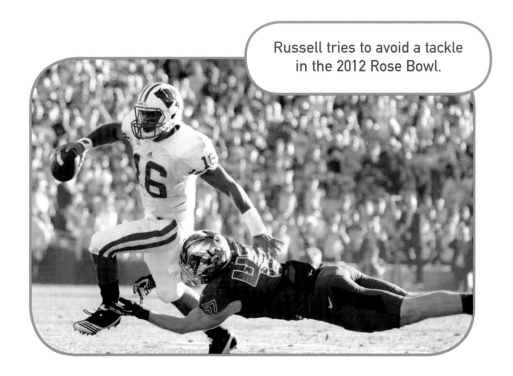

Russell tries to avoid a tackle in the 2012 Rose Bowl.

Russell gives back to his community through Russell Investments. The group supports youth activities in different communities.

Russell had done all he could to prove he was up to playing in the NFL. But many people still had doubts. Before the draft, the official NFL website posted a story about Russell. "At his height, teams will have concerns whether or not he can see to make the throws at the next level," the story said. Shorter quarterbacks sometimes struggle to see over the heads of other players. The article went on to say that a team would probably take Russell in a late round and hope he could "outplay his size."

Rounds 1 and 2 of the 2012 NFL draft went by, and Russell wasn't chosen. Finally, the Seahawks called his name in the third round, after 74 other players were taken. Seattle was thrilled to have him. The team named Russell their starting quarterback.

Russell (*right*) runs for a first down as his teammate Leon Washington (*left*) blocks Eric Berry (*center*) of the Kansas City Chiefs.

Seahawks head coach Pete Carroll gushed about Russell. "He is so prepared," Coach Carroll said. "He doesn't seem like a first-year player." The young quarterback led the Seahawks to a record of 11–5 in 2012. The team eventually fell to the Atlanta Falcons in the **playoffs**.

Everything came together for Russell and the Seahawks in the quarterback's second year. They crushed the Broncos in the 2014 Super Bowl. Russell had proved that he was a special leader at every level. In 2014, he became a champion at the highest level.

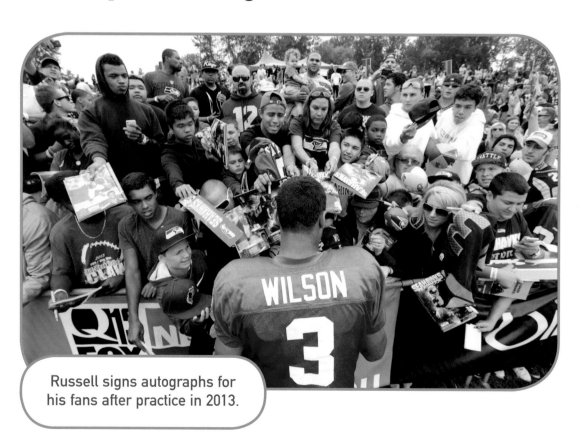

Russell signs autographs for his fans after practice in 2013.

Selected Career Highlights

2013–2014   Led Seattle to a Super Bowl victory
Named to NFL Pro Bowl for
   second time

2012–2013   Became Seattle's starting
   quarterback in first NFL season
Named to NFL Pro Bowl for
   first time

2011–2012   Became Wisconsin's starting
   quarterback in first season with
   the team
Named to All-Big Ten team as one of the
   best players in the Big Ten conference

2010–2011   Named MVP of his team at NC State for second time
Named team captain

2009–2010   Threw 31 touchdown passes, the second most in NC State
   history for a season

2008–2009   Named MVP of his team at NC State for first time
Named Rookie of the Year in his conference

2007–2008   Practiced as a redshirt for NC State

2006–2007   Threw 34 touchdown passes and ran for 18 touchdowns

2005–2006   Threw 40 touchdown passes and ran for 15 touchdowns

2004–2005   Became varsity team's starting quarterback

2003–2004   Started high school at Collegiate School

Glossary

conference: a group of college sports teams that play against one another

defenders: players who try to keep the other team from scoring

degree: a title given to a student after he or she completes an area of study

diabetes: a disease that makes it hard to control the amount of sugar in one's blood

draft: a yearly event in which teams take turns choosing new players from a group

interception: a forward pass that is caught by the other team. The team that catches the interception takes control of the ball.

playoffs: a series of games held to determine a champion

point guard: a basketball player whose main job is to pass the ball

quarterback: a football player whose main job is to throw passes

redshirt: a college athlete who is kept out of competition for a year. Redshirts can extend their time playing sports in college by one year.

shortstop: a baseball player who plays near second base

varsity: the top team at a school

wide receiver: a football player whose main job is to catch passes

Further Reading & Websites

Fishman, Jon M. *Richard Sherman*. Minneapolis: Lerner Publications, 2015.

Kennedy, Mike, and Mark Stewart. *Touchdown: The Power and Precision of Football's Perfect Play*. Minneapolis: Millbrook Press, 2010.

NFL Website
http://www.nfl.com
The NFL's official website provides fans with recent news stories, statistics, biographies of players and coaches, and information about games.

Savage, Jeff. *Peyton Manning*. Minneapolis: Lerner Publications, 2013.

Seattle Seahawks Website
http://www.seahawks.com
The official website of the Seahawks includes team schedules, news, profiles of past and present players and coaches, and much more.

Sports Illustrated Kids
http://www.sikids.com
The *Sports Illustrated Kids* website covers all sports, including football.

LERNER

SOURCE™

Expand learning beyond the printed book. Download free, complementary educational resources for this book from our website, www.lernersource.com.

Index

Photo Acknowledgments

The images in this book are used with the permission of: © The Denver Post/MediaNews Group/Getty Images, pp. 4, 29; © Jamie Squire/Getty Images, p. 5; AP Photo/Seth Wenig, p. 6; © Christian Petersen/Getty Images, p. 7; © Rob Carr/Getty Images, p. 8; © Jamie Squrie/Getty Images, p. 9; Photo courtesy Collegiate School, Richmond, VA. , pp. 10, 15, 16, 17; © iStockphoto .com/bookwyrmm, p. 11; © Richard Stagg/Getty Images, p. 12; © Lance King/Getty Images, p. 19; © G. Fiume/Getty Images, p. 20; AP Photo/Brian Westerholt/Four Seam Images, p. 22; © Joe Robbins/Getty Images, p. 23; © Jonathan Daniel/Getty Images, p. 24; AP Photo/Matt Sayles, p. 25; © Peter G. Aiken/Getty Images, p. 26; AP Photo/Elaine Thompson, p. 28.

Cover: © Justin Edmonds/Getty Images.

Main body text set in Caecilia LT Std 55 Roman 16/28.
Typeface provided by Adobe Systems.